Multiplying

PETER PATILLA

KINGFISHER BOOKS

Kingfisher Books, Grisewood & Dempsey Ltd,
Elsley House, 24–30 Great Titchfield Street,
London W1P 7AD

First published in 1990 by Kingfisher Books

Reprinted 1990

Text Copyright © Peter Patilla 1990
Illustrations copyright © Grisewood and Dempsey Ltd 1990
All rights reserved.
No part of this publication may be reproduced,
stored in a retrieval system or transmitted
by any other means, electronic, mechanical, or
otherwise, without the prior permission of
the publisher.

BRITISH LIBRARY CATALOGUING IN PUBLICATION DATA
Patilla, Peter
Good multiplying.
1. Arithmetic. Multiplication
I. Title   II. McKenna, Terry   III. Series
513.213

ISBN 0-86272-547-X

Editor: John Grisewood

Illustrations: Terry McKenna

Design: Robert Wheeler Design Associates

Phototypeset by Southern Positives and Negatives, (SPAN),
Lingfield, Surrey

Printed in Spain

Contents

Multiplication squares
page 4

Multiplication build up
page 6

Multiplication puzzles
page 8

Investigating with multiplication
page 10

Multiplication patterns
page 12

Multiplication missing numbers
page 14

Calculator multiplication
page 16

Multiplying and large numbers
page 18

Multiplication methods
page 20

Multiplication games
page 22

Multiplication problems
page 24

Measures and multiplying
page 26

Multiplication and data handling
page 28

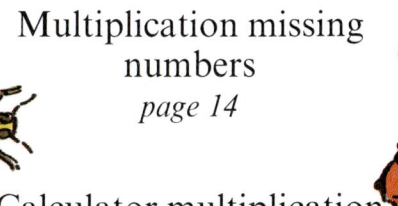

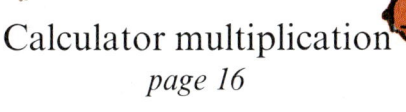

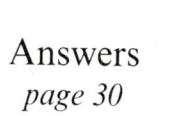

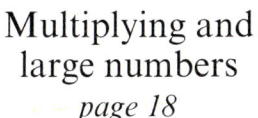

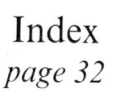

Glossary
page 29

Answers
page 30

Index
page 32

Multiplication squares

Learning your multiplication table facts can be hard work. Here are some activities which may help you understand and enjoy working with tables as well as remembering the answers.

Multiplication Square

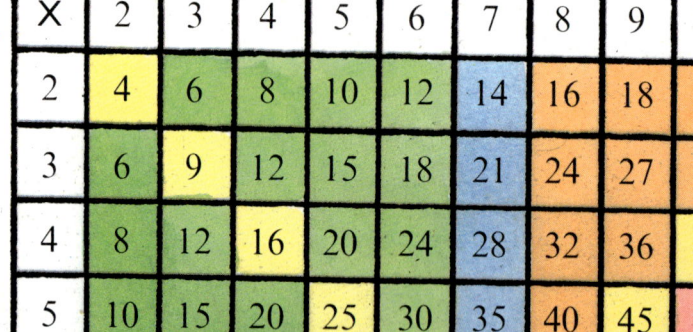

×	2	3	4	5	6	7	8	9	10	11	12
2	4	6	8	10	12	14	16	18	20	22	24
3	6	9	12	15	18	21	24	27	30	33	36
4	8	12	16	20	24	28	32	36	40	44	48
5	10	15	20	25	30	35	40	45	50	55	60
6	12	18	24	30	36	42	48	54	60	66	72
7	14	21	28	35	42	49	56	63	70	77	84
8	16	24	32	40	48	56	64	72	80	88	96
9	18	27	36	45	54	63	72	81	90	99	108
10	20	30	40	50	60	70	80	90	100	110	120
11	22	33	44	55	66	77	88	99	110	121	132
12	24	36	48	60	72	84	96	108	120	132	144

Look at the answers in the green squares. What do you notice?

What do you notice about the answers in the orange, red and brown squares?

Looking for patterns helps you remember facts.

Table Parts

Here are some parts of the multiplication square. Can you work out the missing numbers?

	30
30	

	49	

9

(stepped shape continuing diagonally)

		64		

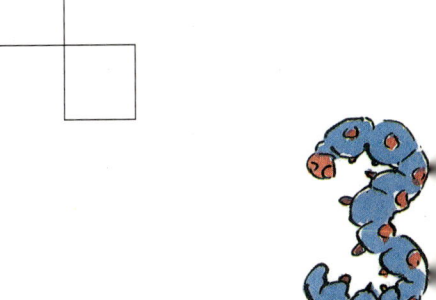

Mini Table Squares

Here are some mini table squares.
What are the missing numbers?

×	2	4	7
3			
5			
6			

×	3	7	
2			20
		42	
8			

×			
	25		
		36	
			49

3 × 2 = 6

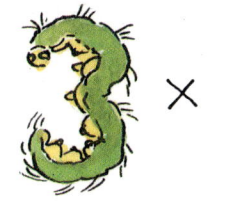

Repeating Answers

Look at all the answers in the large multiplication square. Some answers appear several times in the table. Which answers only appear once in the table?

Multiplication build up

Repeated Addition

Multiplication is a quick way of working out repeated addition.

$5 + 5 + 5 + 5 + 5 + 5$ is the same as 5×6

$2 + 2 + 2$ is the same as 2×3

$13 + 13 + 13 + 13$ is the same as 13×4

Write a multiplication fact to show how many legs there are in each set of these strange insects.

Try to work out the answers to these problems without multiplying!

| $9 \times 15 = 135$ | $4 \times 23 = 92$ | $3 \times 18 = 54$ | $14 \times 20 = 280$ |
| $9 \times 16 = ?$ | $4 \times 25 = ?$ | $3 \times 17 = ?$ | $14 \times 21 = ?$ |

Arrays

Sometimes multiplication is shown in an **array** pattern.
Here are some array patterns.

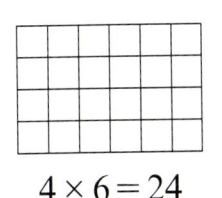

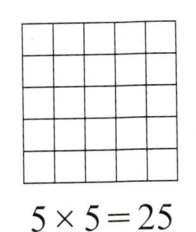

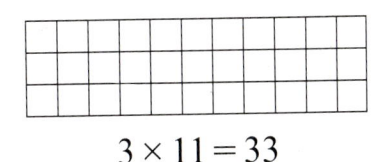

$4 \times 6 = 24$

$5 \times 5 = 25$

$3 \times 11 = 33$

How many beetles in these arrays?

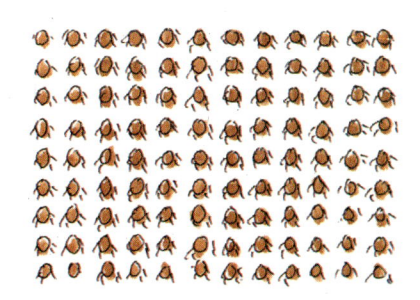

Here are some array patterns for 12.

Can you draw another?

Draw array patterns for... 16 20 30 18 25

Which numbers make square arrays?
Which numbers only make one array?

Multiplication puzzles

Use your multiplication skills to solve these puzzles.

Table Code
Find the answers to each table fact.
Use the code to change answers to letters.
Rearrange the letters to find the names of fruit.

CODE	A	C	E	G	H	L	M	N	O	P	R
	36	49	24	72	35	54	81	63	56	30	64

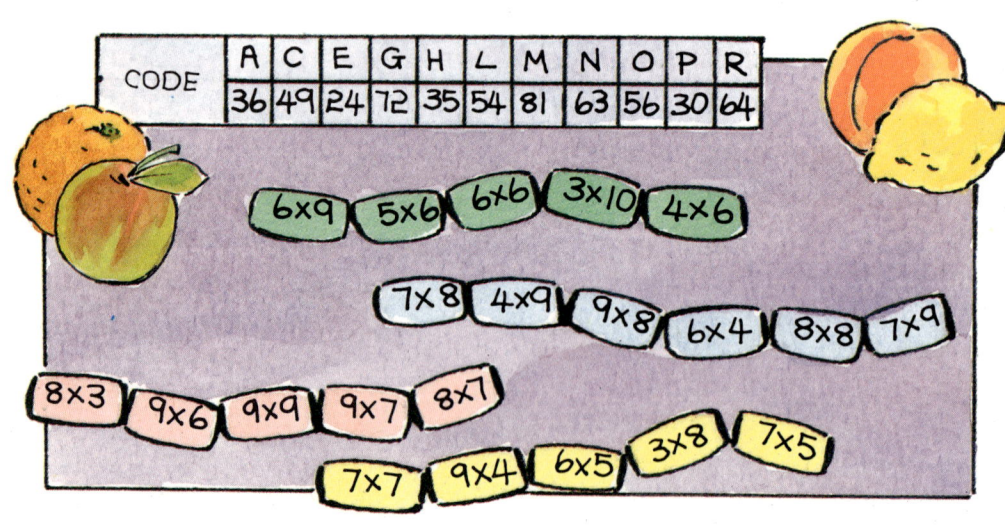

6×9 5×6 6×6 3×10 4×6

7×8 4×9 9×8 6×4 8×8 7×9

8×3 9×6 9×9 9×7 8×7

7×7 9×4 6×5 3×8 7×5

Multiple Honeycomb

The bee can only go into cells which are part of the 6 × table.
Trace routes through the honeycomb.
How many can you find?

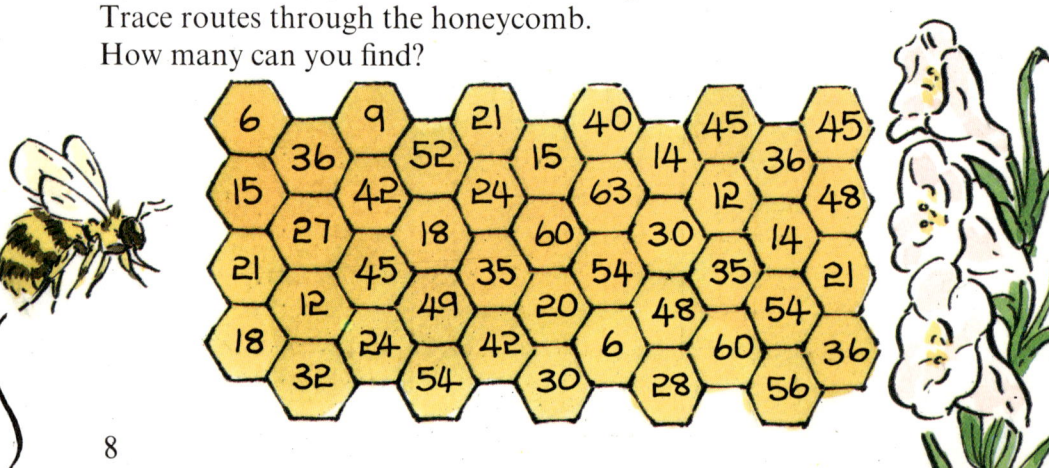

6 9 21 40 45 45
36 52 15 14 36
15 42 24 63 12 48
27 18 60 30 14
21 45 35 54 35 21
12 49 20 48 54
18 24 42 6 60 36
32 54 30 28 56

8

Calculator Puzzle

Calculate 35 × 23.
Turn the calculator upside down to see it cry!

Which multiplications will make these words when the calculator is turned upside down?

BIB   BEE   hOE   ShE

Three Tables Puzzles

Find the numbers which are part of the 3 × table. Write letters which go with the numbers.

Do the same for the 4 × and 5 × tables.

Rearrange the sets of letters to find the names of three farmyard animals.

Table Answer Puzzle

Think of the answers as words and spell them out using the blank spaces.
Find the two mystery animals.

2 × 4 = _ _ _ | _
4 × 3 =   _ _ | _ _ _
5 × 4 = _ _ _ | _ _

4 × 8 =   _ | _ _ _ _ _/_ _ _ _
6 × 7 =   _ | _ _ _ _/_ _ _ _
7 × 9 = _ _ _ _ _/_ _ | _ _
6 × 6 =   _ _ _ _ _/ | _ _
9 × 9 = | _ _ _ _ _ _/_ _ _

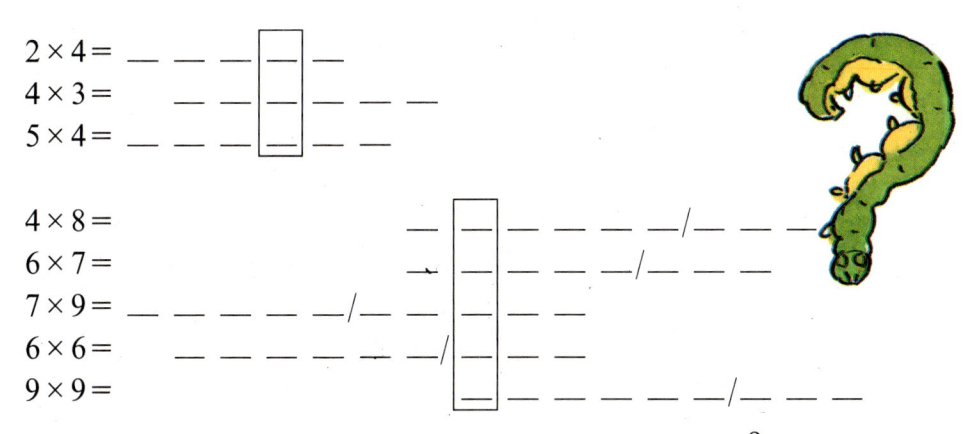

Investigating with multiplication

A square number is a result of multiplying a number by itself.
Here are some square numbers.

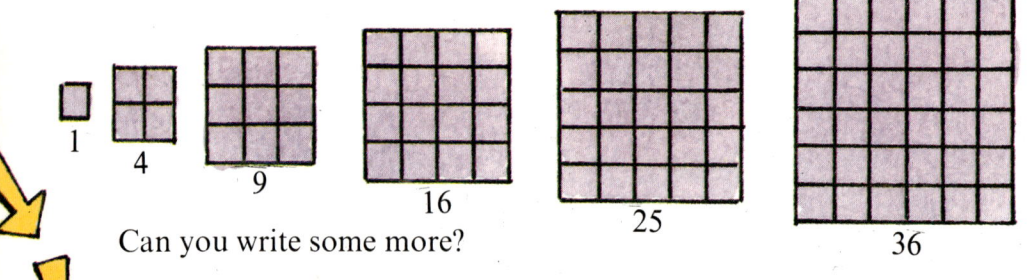

1   4   9   16   25   36

Can you write some more?

Square Numbers Investigation

Use a set of cards which have digits 0–9 written on them.

0 1 2 3 4 5 6 7 8 9

Arrange the cards to make one, two or three digit numbers.
Each number you make must be a square number.

2 5   8 1

Can you use up all the cards?
How many different square numbers can you make?

Calculator Investigation

Use the digit cards 0–9.
Choose any five cards and
arrange them like this

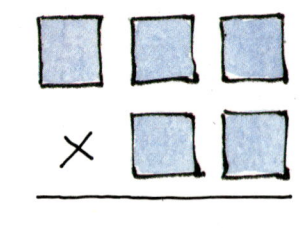

Which arrangement will give
the largest possible answer?

Try with different sets of numbers.

10

Digital roots are found by adding together the digits of a number.

36 [3+6] ➡ 9   42 [4+2] ➡ 6

Sometimes two additions are necessary to find the digital root.

76 [7+6] ➡ 13   [1+3] ➡ 4

Digital Root Investigation

Here are the digital roots of the × 3 and × 9 tables.

	digital root
1 × 3 = 3	3
2 × 3 = 6	6
3 × 3 = 9	9
4 × 3 = 12	3
5 × 3 = 15	6
6 × 3 = 18	9
7 × 3 = 21	3
8 × 3 = 24	6
9 × 3 = 27	9
10 × 3 = 30	3

	digital root
1 × 9 = 9	9
2 × 9 = 18	9
3 × 9 = 27	9
4 × 9 = 36	9
5 × 9 = 45	9
6 × 9 = 54	9
7 × 9 = 63	9
8 × 9 = 72	9
9 × 9 = 81	9
10 × 9 = 90	9

Investigate the digital roots of other tables.

Investigate all the answers of the multiplication tables up to 10 × 10

Table Answers Investigation

The only answer in the nineties is 90.

90 < 9 × 10
     10 × 9

The only answer in the eighties is 80 and 81.

80 < 8 × 10
     10 × 8

Investigate this further.

81 — 9 × 9

11

Multiplication patterns

Multiplication can produce some interesting patterns for you to explore and investigate.

Calculator Pattern
- Start with 37037 on the display.
- Multiply it by 3 and find the digit which is repeated six times.

- Start with 37037 again.
- Multiply it by 5 and find which set of three digits is repeated.

Now you explore multiplying 37037 by any number between 3 and 27 to see what happens.

Table Patterns
Here is a hundred square.

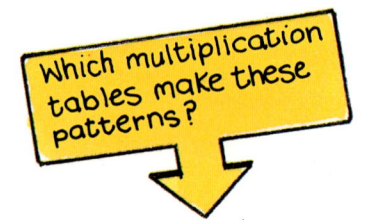

1	2	3	4	5	6	7	8	9	10
11	12	13	14	15	16	17	18	19	20
21	22	23	24	25	26	27	28	29	30
31	32	33	34	35	36	37	38	39	40
41	42	43	44	45	46	47	48	49	50
51	52	53	54	55	56	57	58	59	60
61	62	63	64	65	66	67	68	69	70
71	72	73	74	75	76	77	78	79	80
81	82	83	84	85	86	87	88	89	90
91	92	93	94	95	96	97	98	99	100

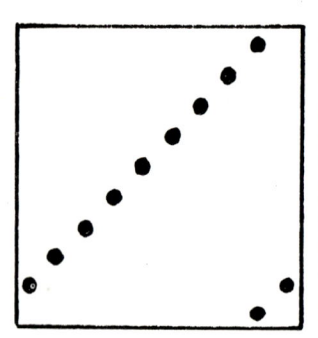

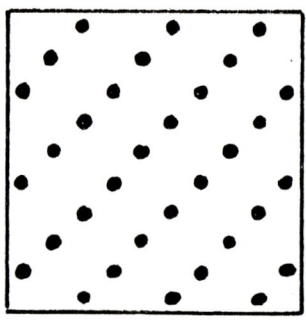

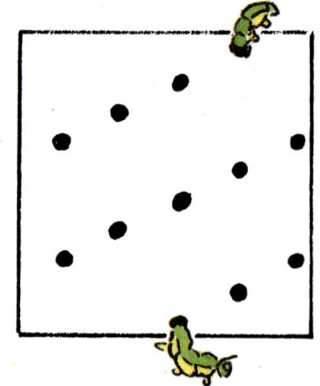

Which multiplication tables make these patterns?

Multiples Patterns

The multiples of **9** are: 9 18 27 36 45 54 63…
Look at the last digit of each number.
What do you notice?

The multiples of **5** are: 5 10 15 20 25 30 35…
Look at the last digit of each number.
What do you notice?

> Investigate the pattern made by the last digit of other multiples.

Special Number Patterns

Multiply 37 by multiples of 3

$$\begin{array}{cccc} 37 & 37 & 37 & 37 \\ \times 3 & \times 6 & \times 9 & \times 12 \end{array}$$

Try other multiples of three.

Why is **37** special?

Is **74** special if you multiply it by multiples of 3?

Commutative Patterns

Multiplication is commutative because the order in which you multiply does not change the answer.

$3 \times 4 = 4 \times 3$

$6 \times 8 = 8 \times 6$

What are the missing numbers?

$5 \times 3 = ? \times 5$

$7 \times 2 = 2 \times ?$

$? \times 4 = ? \times 5$

$? \times 9 = 9 \times 4$

$6 \times ? = 8 \times 6$

Multiplication missing numbers

In these problems some numbers are missing.
Sometimes there will be only one answer.
Other times there will be several possible answers.
Can you discover which is which?

All Square

☐ × ☐ ⇨ 8
× ×
☐ × ☐ ⇨ 18
⇩ ⇩
6 24

☐ × ☐ ⇨ 24
× ×
☐ × ☐ ⇨ 56
⇩ ⇩
21 64

☐ × ☐ ⇨ 30
× ×
☐ × ☐ ⇨ 36
⇩ ⇩
45 24

Equations

4 × ☐ = 36   6 × 5 = ☐   ☐ × 7 = 49   9 × ☐ = 72   ☐ × 8 = 64

Open Equations

☐ × △ = 24   ☐ × △ = 15   ☐ × △ = 81   ☐ × △ = 36

Sequences

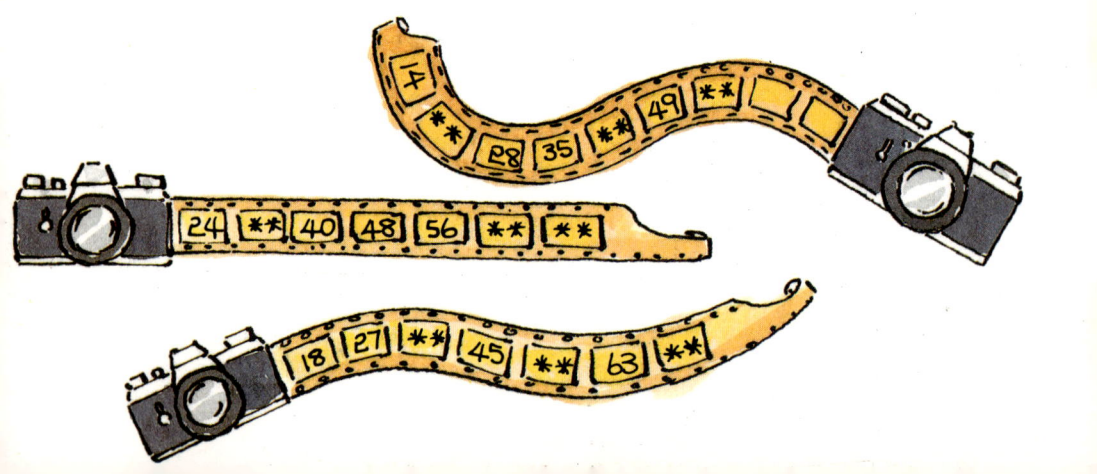

14, **, **, 28, 35, **, 49, **

24, **, 40, 48, 56, **, **

18, 27, **, 45, **, 63, **

Missing Digits

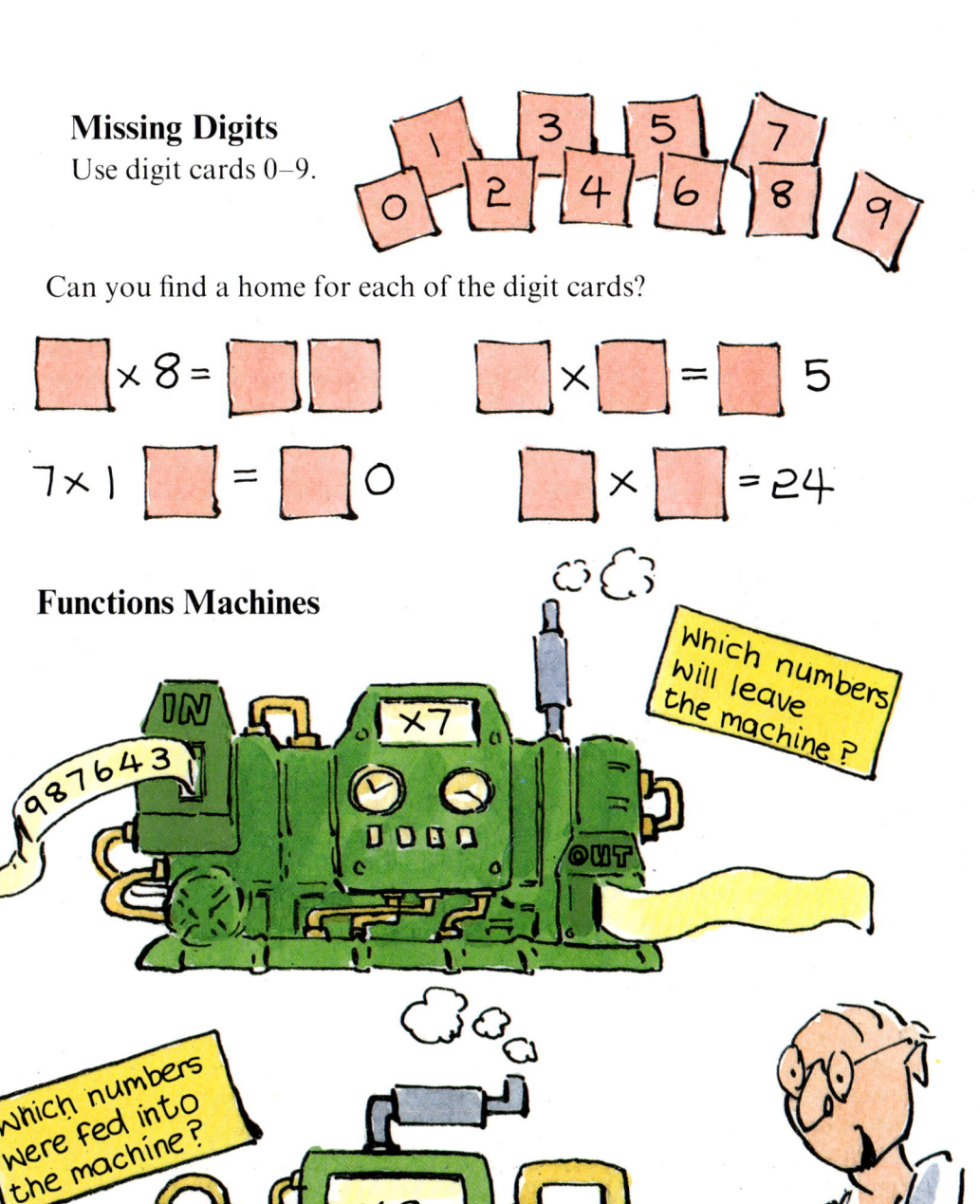

Use digit cards 0–9.

Can you find a home for each of the digit cards?

☐ × 8 = ☐☐   ☐ × ☐ = ☐ 5

7 × 1☐ = ☐ 0   ☐ × ☐ = 24

Functions Machines

×7

987643

Which numbers will leave the machine?

Which numbers were fed into the machine?

×8

IN   OUT   80 72 64 48 40 32

Calculator multiplications

The calculator can be used to help you multiply large numbers. It can also be used to explore and experiment with multiplication of numbers.

Consecutive Numbers

Consecutive numbers are next-door neighbours like:
24 and 25 or 131 and 132

Find which consecutive numbers multiplied together make these answers.

☐ × ☐ = 210.   ☐ × ☐ = 342.

☐ × ☐ = 462.   ☐ × ☐ = 702.

Light Bars

5 × 8 = 40.   The answer of 40 is made from ten light bars.

4 × 8 = 32.   The answer of 32 is also made from ten light bars.

Can you find some multiplications which give answers made from ten light bars?

Forbidden Key

You are not allowed to touch the 2 key.
Here are two ways of finding the answer to 24 × 4 without touching the 2 key.

8 × 3 × 4 =
6 × 4 × 4 =

Can you find any more ways?

Try to find different ways of doing these multiplications without touching the 2 key.

32 × 6

24 × 12

16 × 42

22 × 12

Target

You can only use these number keys.   2 3 4 6 8

You can only use these symbol keys.   × =

Here is one way of hitting the target of 96.

4 × 4 × 6 =   96.

How many different ways can you find of hitting the target of 96?

17

Multiplying and large numbers

Decade Times

Sometimes multiplying large numbers is just as easy as multiplying small numbers.

$4 \times 3 = 12$ $6 \times 8 = 48$
$40 \times 3 = 120$ $60 \times 8 = 480$

Try to answer these in your head.

50×5 70×8
90×3 40×8

3×60 4×70
8×50 7×20

Repeats

12345679 is a very large number!
It uses all the digits except 8.
It is also a special number.
Multiply it by 9, or a multiple of 9 and see why.

15873 is quite a large number.
Multiply it by 7, or a multiple of 7.
Why is it a special number?

15873×7 15873×14 15873×21

Russian Multiplication

Many years ago Russian peasants used a method of multiplying which only used adding, halving and doubling.
This is how it worked to answer 46 × 35.

STEP 1
Halve left column and ignore any remainder

Stop at 1

46	×	35
23		70
11		140
5		280
2		560
1		1120

Double right hand column

STEP 2
Cross out all Even numbers on left column and....

Cross out the corresponding number in the right column

STEP 3
Add the numbers remaining in the right column

~~46~~	×	~~35~~
23		70
11		140
5		280
~~2~~		~~560~~
1		1120
		1610

Try this method with some long multiplications of your own.

Quick Thinking

Which of these numbers can be changed to 5000 using multiplication only?

25   30   16   75   48

Multiplication methods

There are many different methods of working out the answers to multiplication problems.
Try some of these methods.

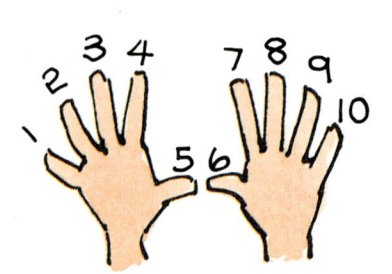

Finger Tables
Your fingers can be numbered like this. They can now be used to help you answer the 9 × table.

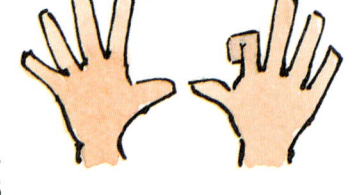

To find the answer to 9 × 7 hold down the seventh finger. There are six fingers to the left and three fingers to the right.
9 × 7 = 63

Which 9 × table fact do these hands show? Try some of your own.

Quick Elevens
Here is a quick way of multiplying by 11.

Try some 11× of your own

1 Write down the units digit.

2 Add each digit to its neighbour.

3 Write down the first digit.

$$435 \times 11$$
$$\overline{5}$$

$$435 \times 11$$
$$\overline{85}$$

$$435 \times 11$$
$$\overline{785}$$

$$435 \times 11$$
$$\overline{4785}$$

立 尺 吉 心

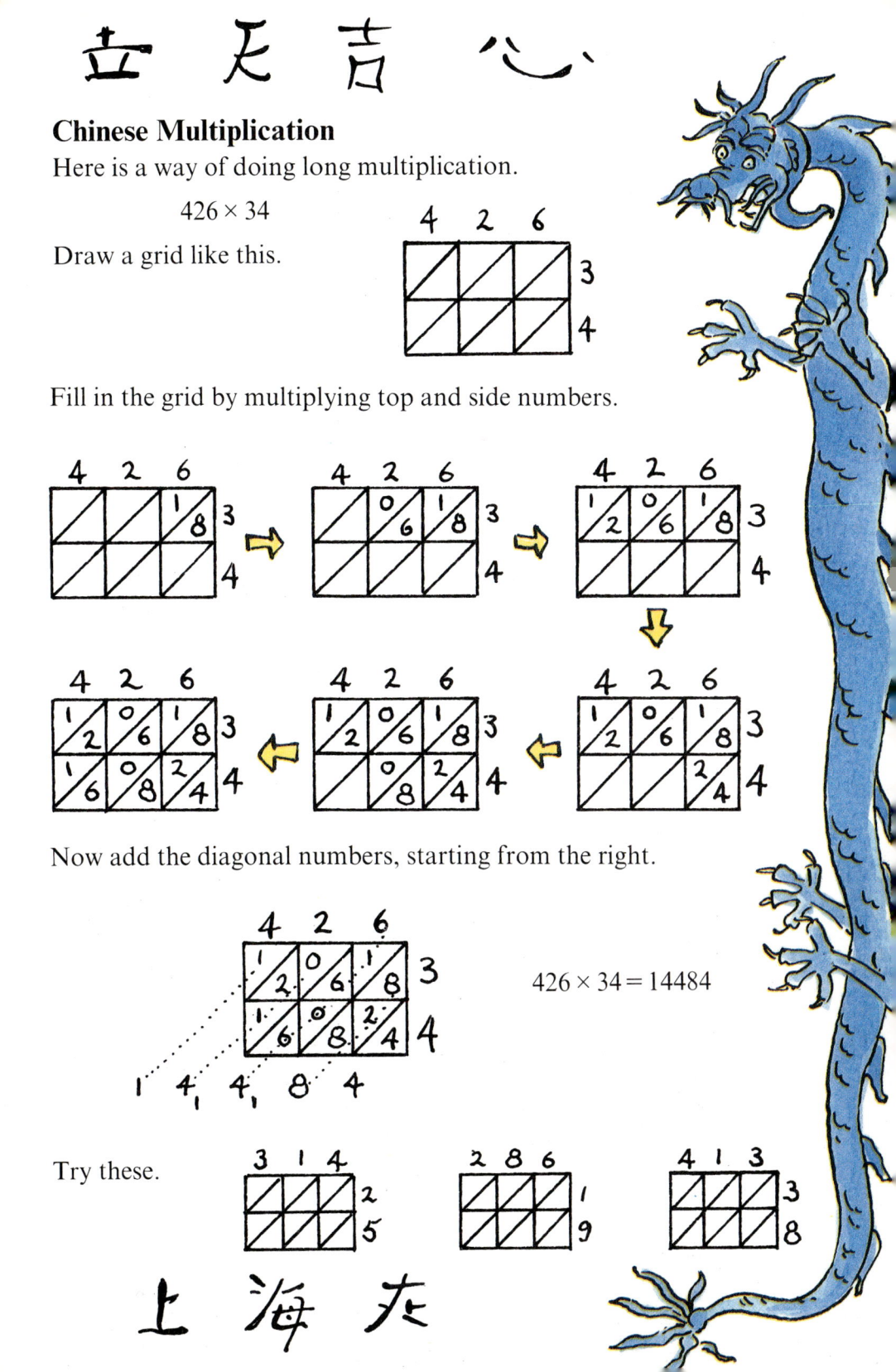

Chinese Multiplication

Here is a way of doing long multiplication.

426 × 34

Draw a grid like this.

Fill in the grid by multiplying top and side numbers.

Now add the diagonal numbers, starting from the right.

426 × 34 = 14484

Try these.

Multiplication games

Use your multiplication skills to play these games.

Patience

Use a deck of playing cards without the pictures.
Deal four cards face up and place the rest face down.
One card at a time is turned over from the deck.
This card can be placed below any of the face up cards.
When a column adds up to a multiple of 10 it can be removed.
Can you remove all the columns before the deck runs out?

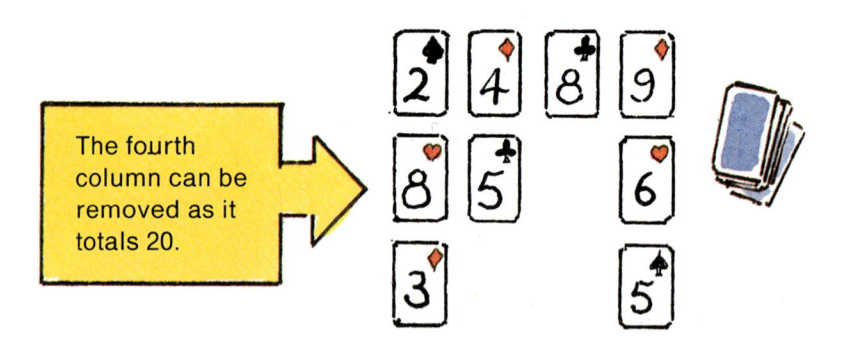

The fourth column can be removed as it totals 20.

Multiples

3	6	12	6	24
18	12	9	12	18
6	12	6	36	12
30	18	6	12	18
18	6	18	15	6

A game for two players.
Take turns to roll a dice.
One player multiplies their score by 3 and covers the answer on the board.
The other player multiplies their score by 6 and covers the answer on the board.

Game 1: Try to cover the most numbers.
Game 2: Try to get three of your markers in a straight line.

Dominoes

Make a square with dominoes.
The total of each side
must be a multiple of 5.
How many squares can you make?
Can you make squares
whose side totals are multiples of 4?

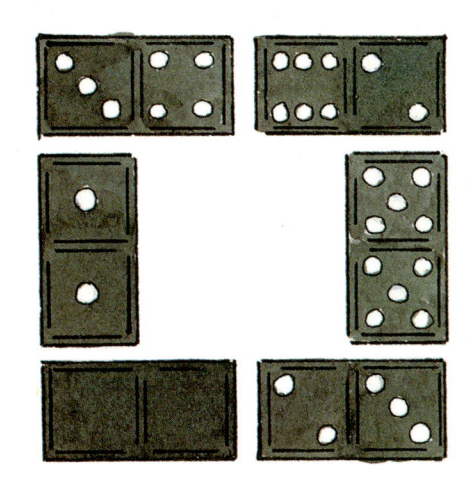

Hex

Each player is trying to make a chain of their markers across the board.
The chain can be from side to side or top to bottom.
Multiply any two red digits together to cover an appropriate hexagon number.
A digit can be multiplied by itself.

Multiplication problems

Some multiplication problems are simple and straight forward, others are there to make you think.
See how you get on with these problems.

Operations Problem

You may use a calculator if you wish.

Digits which must be used.   **2 4 6 8**

Operations which must be used   × × +

$4 \times 2 \times 8 + 6 = 70$

Problems

What is the largest answer you can make?

What is the smallest answer you can make?

Can you make an answer of exactly 100?

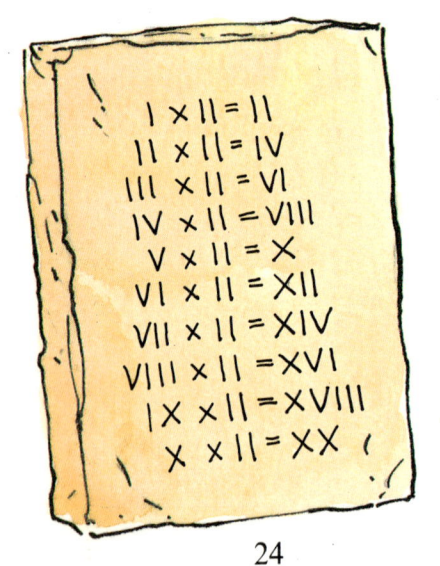

Roman Problem

If you think multiplying is tricky think of the poor Roman children learning their tables!

Write out the 4× table as a Roman child would have done.

How would they have tackled this multiplication?

$$\begin{array}{r} XIV \\ \times\ V \\ \hline \end{array}$$

I × II = II
II × II = IV
III × II = VI
IV × II = VIII
V × II = X
VI × II = XII
VII × II = XIV
VIII × II = XVI
IX × II = XVIII
X × II = XX

Numbers Problem

Use the digits **3 6 8** and the × sign.
Make all the different multiplication problems you can with them.
Here are two to start you off:

   $3 \times 6 \times 8$ 68×3

There are five more for you to find.
Which gives the biggest answer?

Abacus Problem

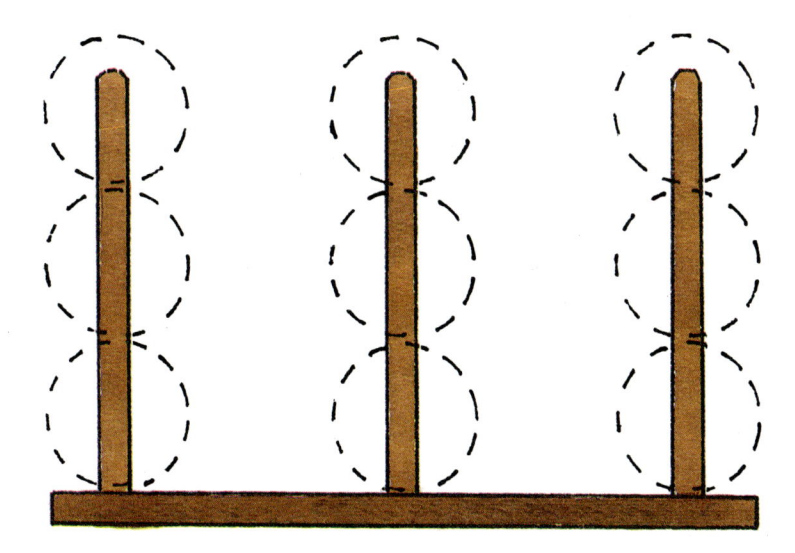

Place 3 small coins on the abacus to show numbers.

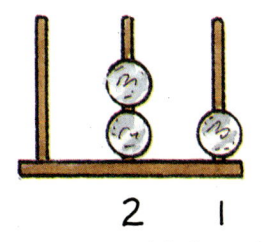

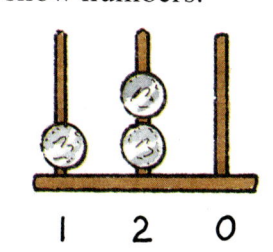

2 1

1 2 0

How many multiples of 3 can you show?
Can you make a number which is not a multiple of 3?

Measures and multiplying

Multiplication skills are needed when we use measures.

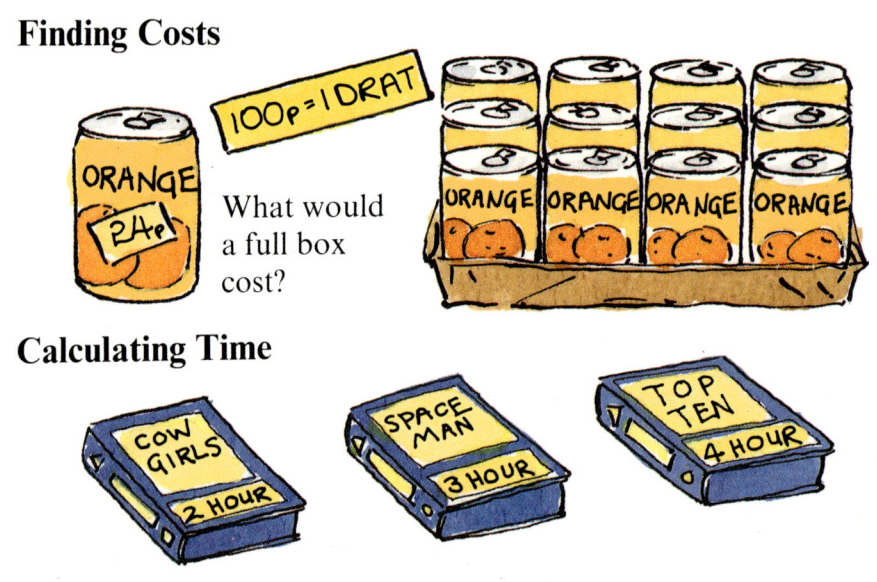

Finding Costs

100p = 1 DRAT

ORANGE 24p

What would a full box cost?

Calculating Time

COW GIRLS 2 HOUR

SPACE MAN 3 HOUR

TOP TEN 4 HOUR

How many minutes would each tape last?

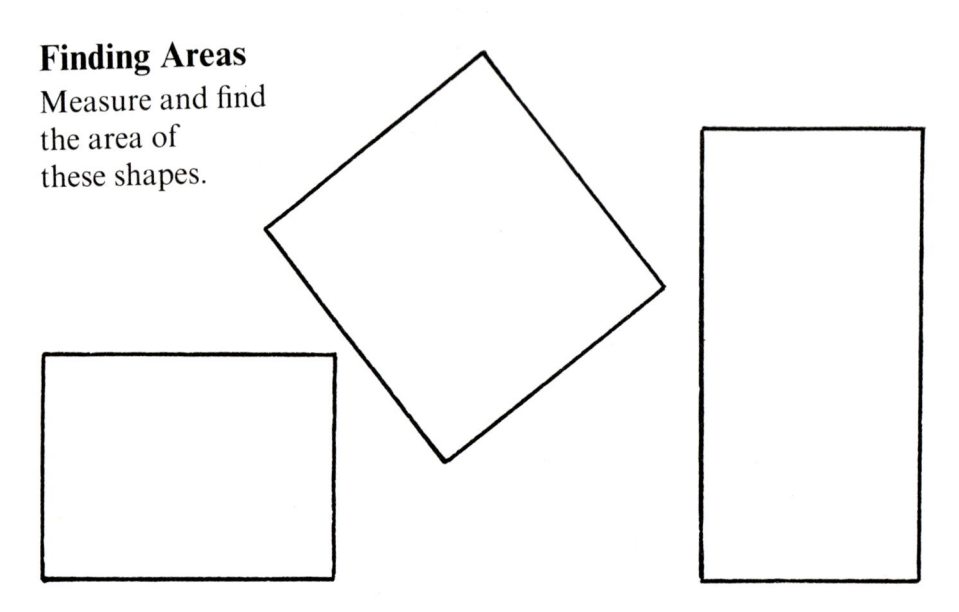

Finding Areas

Measure and find the area of these shapes.

Calculating Weight

What will be the weight of 6 packets?

Calculating Quantity

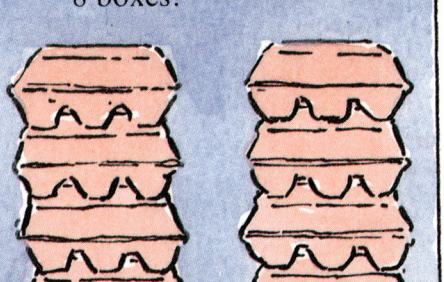

How many eggs in 8 boxes?

Calculating Capacity

What is the total capacity of 10 bottles?

Calculating Length

Each fence panel is 90cm long.
How far would seven such panels stretch?

Multiplication and data handling

Information is presented to us in all sorts of ways:

Use your skills to find the answers to these Venn diagram problems.

Use the numbers 1 to 30. Copy the Venn diagrams and write where you think the numbers 1–30 go on each one.

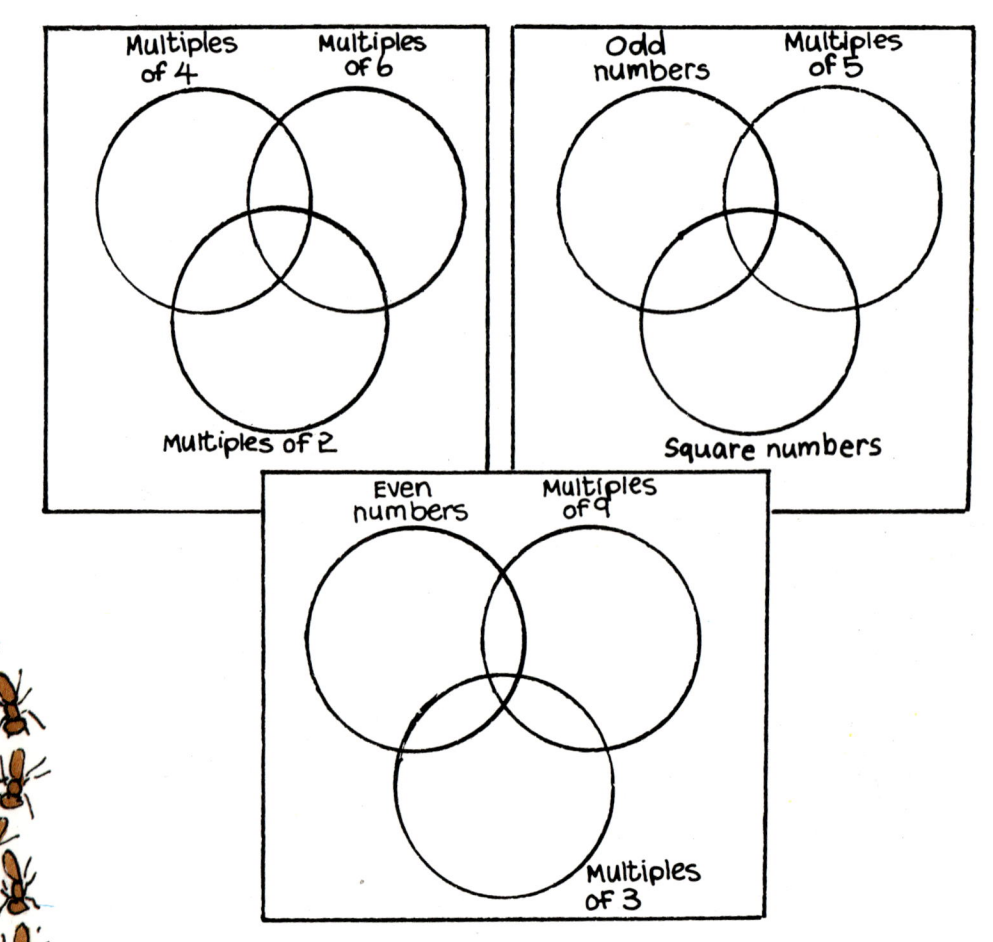

Diagram 1: Multiples of 4, Multiples of 6, Multiples of 2

Diagram 2: Odd numbers, Multiples of 5, Square numbers

Diagram 3: Even numbers, Multiples of 9, Multiples of 3

28

Glossary

Arrays: Patterns arranged in rows and columns.

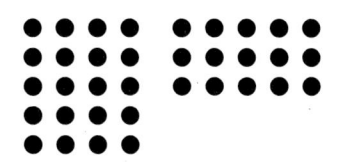

```
● ● ● ●    ● ● ● ● ●
● ● ● ●    ● ● ● ● ●
● ● ● ●    ● ● ● ● ●
● ● ● ●
```

Commutative: Multiplication is commutative because the order in which you multiply it makes no difference to the answer.
$3 \times 6 = 6 \times 3$
Addition is also commutative.
$4 + 6 = 6 + 4$
Subtraction and division are not commutative.

Consecutive numbers: These are numbers which follow on from each other e.g. 10, 11, 12 and 56, 57, 58, 59.

Digits: The digits are: 0, 1, 2, 3, 4, 5, 6, 7, 8, 9.
Some numbers have two digits (35, 78, 95).
Some numbers have three digits (108, 567, 856).

Digital root: Digital root is the digit obtained by adding together the separate digits of a number.
24 .. (2 + 4 = 6) .. digital root is 6.
67 .. (6 + 7 = 13) .. (1 + 3 = 4) .. digital root is 4.

Even Numbers: Numbers which can be divided exactly by two.
Here are some even numbers: 2, 6, 18, 74, 90, 142.

Multiples: The multiples of 2 are 2 4 6 8 10 12 ...
The multiples of 3 are 3 6 9 12 15 18 ...
The multiples of 4 are 4 8 12 16 20 24 ...

Odd Numbers: Numbers which cannot be divided by two without leaving a remainder.
Here are some odd numbers: 3, 5, 27, 41, 89, 125.

Square Numbers: A square number is obtained by multiplying a number by itself.
36 is a square number because $6 \times 6 = 36$.
81 is a square number because $9 \times 9 = 81$.

Sum: To sum a set of numbers means to add them together. The sum of 12, 20 and 34 is 66.

Total: To total a set of numbers means to add them together. The total of 12, 20 and 34 is 66.

Answers

Page 5
Table parts

25	30
30	36

42	49	56
48	56	64

9

16

25

40	48	56	64	72	80

Mini table squares

×	2	4	7
3	6	12	21
5	10	20	35
6	12	24	42

×	3	7	10
2	6	14	20
6	18	42	60
8	24	56	80

×	5	6	7
5	25	30	35
6	30	36	42
7	35	42	49

Repeating answers
4 9 25 49 64 81 100 121 144

Page 6
Repeated addition
$8 \times 9 = 72$ $6 \times 7 = 42$ $4 \times 6 = 24$

$9 \times 15 = 135$ $4 \times 23 = 92$
$9 \times 16 = 144$ $4 \times 25 = 100$
$3 \times 18 = 54$ $14 \times 20 = 280$
$3 \times 17 = 51$ $14 \times 21 = 294$

Page 7
Arrays
54   36   108
16 and 25 make square arrays.
25 only makes one array.

Page 8
Table code
APPLE   ORANGE

LEMON (or MELON) PEACH

Multiple honeycomb
There are four routes

Page 9
Three tables puzzles
MOUSE   HORSE   GOOSE

Table answer puzzle
HEN   HORSE

Page 12
Table patterns
9×   3×   8×

Commutative pattern
$5 \times 3 = 3 \times 5$ $7 \times 2 = 2 \times 7$
$5 \times 4 = 4 \times 5$ $4 \times 9 = 9 \times 4$
$6 \times 8 = 8 \times 6$

Page 14
All square

2	4
3	6

3	8
7	8

5	6
9	4

Equations
$4 \times 9 = 36$ $6 \times 5 = 30$ $7 \times 7 = 49$
$9 \times 8 = 72$ $8 \times 8 = 64$

Open equations
There are several answers to each equation.
24 = (1 × 24) (2 × 12) (3 × 8) (4 × 6) (6 × 4) (8 × 3) (12 × 2) (24 × 1)

15 = (1 × 15) (3 × 5) (5 × 3) (15 × 1)

81 = (1 × 81) (3 × 27) (9 × 9) (27 × 3) (81 × 1)

36 = (1 × 36) (2 × 18) (3 × 12) (4 × 9) (6 × 6) (9 × 4) (12 × 3) (18 × 2) (36 × 1)

Sequences
14 21 28 35 42 49 56 63 70
24 32 40 48 56 64 72
18 27 36 45 54 63 72

Page 15
Missing digits
2 × 8 = 16   9 × 5 = 45
7 × 10 = 70   8 × 3 = 24

Function machine
out: 21 28 42 49 56 63
in: 4   5   6   8   9   10

Page 16
Consecutive numbers
14 × 15 = 210   18 × 19 = 342
21 × 22 = 462   26 × 27 = 702

Light bars
There are many answers
(e.g. 8 × 8   7 × 10)

Page 19
Quick thinking
25

Page 20
Finger tables
3 × 9   9 × 9   4 × 9

Page 24
Operations problem
Largest: 2 + 4 × 8 × 6 = 288

Smallest: 6 × 4 × 2 + 8 = 56

100 = 8 × 6 × 2 + 4

Page 25
Numbers problem
3 × 6 × 8   36 × 8   63 × 8   86 × 3

68 × 3   83 × 6   38 × 6

The biggest answer is 63 × 8 = 504

Abacus problem
3 12 21 30 102 111 120 201 210 300
All the numbers will be multiples of 3.

Page 26
Finding costs
288p (2.88 Drats)

Calculating time
120min   180min   240min

Finding areas
12cm^2 16cm^2 18cm^2

Page 27
Calculating weight
2520g (2.520kg)

Calculating quantity
48

Calculating capacity
2500ml (2.5l)

Calculating length
630cm (6.3m)

31

Page 28
Venn diagrams

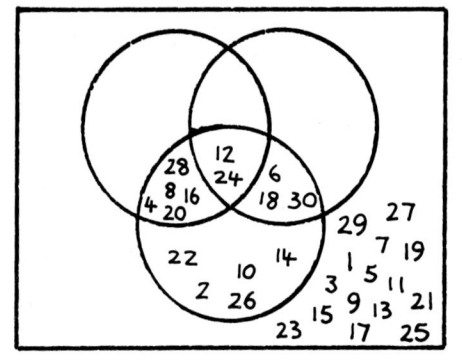

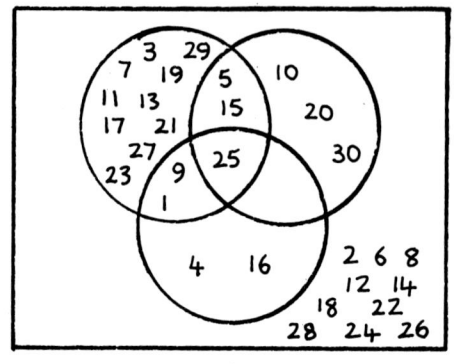

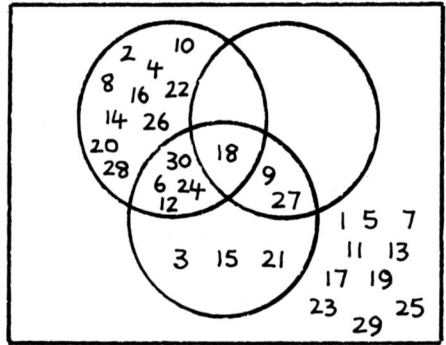

Index

Abacus 25
Answers 30
Area 26
Arrays 7, 26
Calculator 9, 10, 12, 16, 17, 24
Capacity 27
Codes 8, 9
Commutative 13
Consecutive 16
Data 28
Digit cards 10, 15
Digital roots 11
Digits 10, 11, 12, 15, 18, 23, 24, 25
Equations 6, 13, 14, 15
Even numbers 28
Functions 15
Games 22, 23
Glossary 29
Grids 4, 5, 7, 8, 12, 21, 22, 23

Investigations 7, 10, 11, 16, 17, 23, 24, 25
Length 27
Measures 26, 27
Missing numbers 5, 6, 9, 13, 14, 15, 16
Money 26
Multiples 13, 18, 22, 25, 28
Multiplication squares 4, 5, 12
Multiplication methods 19, 20, 21, 24
Odd numbers 28
Patterns 4, 5, 7, 12, 13, 18
Problems 15, 16, 17, 24, 25, 26, 27
Puzzles 8, 9
Repeated addition 6, 26, 27
Sequences 14
Square numbers 7, 10, 28
Time 26
Venn diagrams 28
Weight 27